STALINGRAD

FIRST PUBLISHED IN GREAT BRITAIN IN 2001 BY CAXTON EDITIONS
AN IMPRINT OF CAXTON PUBLISHING GROUP
20 BLOOMSBURY STREET, LONDON WC1 3QA

© CAXTON EDITIONS, 2001.

ISBN 1 84067 152 1

A COPY OF THE CIP DATA IS AVAILABLE FROM THE
BRITISH LIBRARY UPON REQUEST.

REPROGRAPHICS BY GA GRAPHICS
PRINTED AND BOUND BY
APP PRINTING

ACKNOWLEDGMENTS:
WITH THANKS TO
TRH PICTURES AND AKG LONDON

RUSSIAN TRANSLATIONS BY NICK HEARN

STALINGRAD

A PICTORIAL HISTORY

CAXTON EDITIONS

INTRODUCTION

THE FIGHT FOR STALINGRAD in 1942-43 was a great turning point in the Second World War as for first time the German Army was comprehensively defeated, so destroying the myth of Nazi invincibility. After Stalingrad, German expansionism was over, with defeats coming in North Africa and Italy, they now slowly began to retreat on all fronts until their eventual capitulation in May 1945.

The name 'Stalingrad' became an obsession with Hitler. It overshadowed his strategic objective of gaining access to the Caucasian oil fields, which he saw as essential in supplying fuel for the Nazi military machine and depriving the Soviets of their resources. Hitler insisted in taking complete control of the campaign, ignoring his generals more pragmatic approach. Refusing all notions of making tactical with-drawals, Hitlers stubbornness resulted in the annihilation of the whole of his 6th Army.

Stalingrad was a battle fought between two totalitarian dictators, neither of whom had any regard for their own men, nor would countenance any possibility of retreat. Their troops were told to fight to the death. Such was the ferocity of the engagement, that at the end of the battle, no building in Stalingrad remained intact.

Hitler had revealed his aggressive ambitions for a German empire in the east in the 1920s in his book *Mein Kampf*. The push eastwards began the Second World War, with the German invasion of Poland in September 1939 and continued with Operation Barbarossa, the attack on the Soviet Union in June 1941, which stunned Stalin, who thought he had an non-aggression pact with Hitler.

The ease with which the Nazis had invaded Western Europe, had made Hitler overconfident. The Nazis completely underestimated the Russian terrain, weather conditions, infrastructure, numerical odds of the Red Army and Soviet's manufacturing capabilities.

Although Hitler's generals had favoured a renewed attack on Moscow, after the initial success of the invasion, Hitler wanted access to the Caucasian oil-fields and hoped to encircle Moscow later. This resulted in the Nazi military capability being split and one of the most brutal conflicts the world has ever seen take place. Two personalities dominated this titanic struggle: Adolf Hitler and Josef Stalin.

HITLER

HITLER FIRST MADE KNOWN HIS INTENTION to expand a German empire eastwards in his autobiography, *Mein Kampf.* Written in prison in the early 1920's, after the failed Beer Hall Putsch, the book also clearly outlined his hatred for Jews, communism and the Slavic peoples.

When he came into power in 1933, this threat to Russia increasingly became more probable. Stalin was acutely aware of this and took great measures to appease Hitler, eagerly signing a non-aggression 10 year Nazi-Soviet Pact in 1939. Many were surprised at this pact, knowing Hitler was politically, at the other end of the spectrum. In hindsight, this was just a ploy to enable Hitler to invade Poland more easily and with with the help of the Russians. He had no intention of keeping to the pact and secretly was binding his time and building up his troops behind the Russian border.

The successful conquest of Russia was to provide Germany with *Lebensraum*, or living space for the intended expansion of the Aryan population. Most importantly, it would also give the agricultural and industrial infrastructure needed for Hitler's global ambitions. These lands were to be acquired by force and at the expense of the Slavic nations, including Russians, who were to be removed, enslaved, or eliminated. As well as destroying the only military power capable of challenging him, it would also rid the world of what he called the 'Jewish Bolshevik gang'.

Hitler with Albert Speer in Paris after the fall of France in 1940. He was soon to turn his attentions to Russia.

STALIN

JOSEPH STALIN was born 21 December 1879 as Josef Vissarionovich Djugashvili, in the provincial Georgian town of Gori in the Caucasus, which was then an imperial Russian colony. His father was poor shoemaker and a drunk who regularly beat him and his mother, a devout washer-woman, who wanted her son to become a priest.

To this end he studied at the Tiflis Theology Seminary but left without graduating to become a full time revolutionary organiser. He was a member of the Georgian branch of the Social Democratic party in 1901, encouraging workers to strike and spreading socialist literature. When the party split into two groups, Stalin supported the more radical Bolsheviks and their leader Vladimir Lenin. He rapidly gained influence and power within the party.

Stalin appeared outwardly modest and unassuming and it was easy for his opponents to underestimate him. Possessing no oratorical skills or charisma, his talents lay in applying shrewd practical intelligence to political organisation. He became the new soviet leader after Lenin's death in 1924. He then manipulated and gradually controlled all aspects of the communist party .

In the late 20s' and 30's he pushed for industrialisation faster than anyone believed possible. This involved, in 1929, the disastrous start of forced collective farming. Anyone who resisted including 'Kulaks', a bolshevik term for a middle-class farmer was 'liquidated'. By 1933, the harvests had failed and millions died through starvation. From 1934-1936 he began the great purges arresting virtually all major party figures. By 1939, 98 of the 139 central committee members had been shot and 1,108 out of 1,966 delegates of the 17th

A formal portrait of Stalin

Congress had been arrested. While this was happening Stalin

promoted a cult of popular adulation.

Soviet Molotov signs the Non-Aggression Pact, Stalin and Ribbentrop are in the background.

Towards the end of the 30's Stalin made unsuccessful attempts to reach an accord with Western democracies. He did conclude a non-aggression treaty with Hitler on August the 23rd in 1939. Known as the Nazi-Soviet pact, it was signed by Molotov for the Soviet Union and Ribbentrop for the Nazis. The pact was supposed to ensure non-aggression between the two signatories for 10 years. A secret protocol allowed for the division of Poland and the Baltic states between the two states.

This allowed Hitler to invade Poland without having to fight a war on two fronts. When he invaded Poland he knew that he would not have to fight Russia. He knew that he may have to fight France and Britain if they honoured their guarantees, but this would only be when he had secured Poland.

Hitler meets Molotov.

Nazi troops march through Warsaw.

POLAND

ON SEPTEMBER 1ST 1939, Hitler invaded Poland with his highly developed military machine in what became known as a 'blitzkrieg' (lightning war). His high-speed panzer tanks units moved quickly across the country.

The advance into Poland was the start of the Second World War when Britain and France declared war on Germany on 3rd September, 1939. Although the Polish lancers on horse-back bravely counter attacked, they stood no chance against superior armoury. The German Luftwaffe destroyed the Polish airforce and destroyed communications which disrupted their ability to bring reinforcements, ammunitions and supplies to the front lines. Bombs were then dropped on defenceless Polish cities.

The Polish army had 800,000 men, 225 small tanks and 313 obsolete aircraft. The Germans had 1,512,000 troops, 2,977 tanks and 1,300 modern aircraft. On the 17th September the Soviets invaded the east of Poland. Within 28 days of the invasion, 10,572 Germans were killed. 30,322 wounded and 3,409 missing. 2,93 % of the total fighting force.

On September 17th Soviet troops also invaded Poland from the east and next day the Polish government and high command escaped into exile. The USSR occupied the eastern half with Ukranians and white Russians. the Germans took the western half including Gdansk (Danzig) and also the Polish corridor. Stalin also forced the three Baltic States, Estonia, Lithuania and Latvia to be incorporated into the USSR.

On 27 September, German artillery entered Warsaw.

After the invasion of Poland, Reinhard Heydrich, who was second in command of the SS, systematically organised the mass murder of large sections of the Polish population. Later, the Nazi occupied Soviet Union was to experience a similar terror.

Herman Göering, commander of the Luftwaffe.

Stalin then tried to force Finland with whom he also had a non-aggression pact to become integrated in the Soviet Union. Finland resisted and the USSR denounced its non-aggression pact and invaded on 28th November 1939.

The Finns put up strong resistance and it was only the USSRs greater number of soldiers which forced the Finns to give away strategic ports, airports and a navel base.

After the defeat of France, and when Britain was not an immediate military threat, Hitler set his sights once again in the east, on to the USSR which he saw as a means of providing him with an empire. He had long despised the Slavic peoples and intended them to become servants and slaves to resettled German colonies.

Preparations for the great offensive against the USSR code-named Barbarossa had actually begun as early as December 1940. He had hoped to make peace with Britain because he did not want to fight a war on two fronts. However after losing the battle of Britain, he decided to put the British invasion on hold, and use all his energies and military power to conquer the east.

He first scheduled an attack for the middle of May, 1941, but delayed the assault as his campaign in the Balkans was underway.

Hitler knew that his army would be numerically disadvantaged but this aspect had not stopped their recent successes on the battlefield. When the Germans invaded France, they were outnumbered. The French, Dutch, Belgian and British armies had a combined force of 3,740,000 to 2,760,000: an advantage of 980,000 men. They

Winston Churchill, who became Prime Minister of Great Britain after the fall of Poland, and who agreed to be an ally of Stalin after the attack on Russia.

also had more tanks and a superiority in artillery. Only in aircraft did the Germans have a distinct and decisive advantage, having a superiority of 1,134 machines.

Within nine months, Germany had conquered Poland, Norway, Denmark, Holland, Belgium, Luxembourg and France. All attacks were fast and decisive and the losses of German lives were light. The intoxicating effect of easy victory on Hitler and his generals, sowed the seeds for future over-ambition which were to have far-reaching effects on their planning of Barbarossa.

German artillery enters Warsaw on 27 September, 1939, after aerial and artillery bombardment.

STALINGRAD

The Germans attack Russia.

BARBAROSSA

ON EARLY SUNDAY morning 22 June 1941, Operation Barbarossa began. 3,050,000 German troops along with pro-Axis troops from Rumania, Austria and Italy bringing a total of 4 million, had amassed on the Soviet border. Hitler wished to establish a line from the Volga river to Archangel. The Luftwaffe were to then finish off the last of Russia's industry in the Urals. The huge build up was mainly in East Prussia and the Polish border and was under radio silence. Right up to the last, many German soldiers believed that it was all part of an elaborate diversion to the real plan which was to invade Britain.

He launched another Blitzkrieg with 121 divisions on a 3,200 kilometre front (2,000 miles), from the Black Sea to the

Baltic. In the north, the Germans moved towards Leningrad via the Baltic states. In the centre the target was Moscow via Smolensk. In the south the Germans marched towards the Ukraine and Kiev. They intended to then turn south to the the Crimea and cross the river Don on to the Caucasus and then on to Stalingrad by the river Volga. A further, smaller force of Germans and Rumanians went south.

Hitler thought that the whole communist edifice would come 'crashing to the ground' once attacked, as it was 'rotten to the core.' This view was widely shared amongst many foreign observers as Stalin's purges, which began in 1937 had dismissed, imprisoned or executed 36,671 officers. Of 706 officers of the rank of Brigade Commander and above, over 400 had been persecuted. Russia's war against Finland in 1939-40, suggested that it was only their vast numerical strength which won through.

After an initial speedy advance, the Germans became enmeshed in the Russian roads and weather.

Panzer divisions travelled many miles in the initial advance.

Exhausted German troops rest against a Pzkpfw IV.

Hitler's pretext for invading was that the Soviets were planning an invasion themselves. This was completely false as the Soviets were surprised and shocked when the Germans crossed their border.

In Berlin, the Russian Ambassadors Dekanozov and Berezhkov were summoned by Joachim von Ribbentrop and told 'The Soviet Government's hostile attitude to Germany and the serious threat represented by Russian troop concentrations on Germany's eastern frontier have compelled the Reich to take counter-measures. The Führer has charged me with informing you officially of these defensive measures.'

When the they returned to their Embassy they found that their telephone wires had been cut. Turning to their radio they tuned in to Moscow they found, to their surprise, that no mention was made of the invasion.

Germans killed in attack from partisans. From the early days of the war partisan groups set-up behind German lines. Their fought bravely against superior odds.

Bread being brought to partisans hiding in the marshes.

The penalty for aiding partisans was summary execution.

Nazis murdered Communists, Jews and Partisans on a massive scale. Their murderous barbarity alienated many people of Stalin's regime who had first welcomed Hitler's troops as liberators.

39

Soviet partisans consisted of three groups. The first were the resistance group well run by key members of the communist party. The second group were bitter civilians forced out of their homes by German troops, who had often witnessed relatives being killed or taken and used for slave labour. Fearing the same fate, they hid and then later became partisans. The last group were the large number of Red Army troops who broke out of encirclement and escaped into hiding.

All those suspected of being partisans were treated harshly and executed, regardless of their age. This treatment was counter-productive as it only increased support for partisan groups, encouraging even more guerrilla attacks upon the Germans.

Moscow, November 1941, the Russian winter has set in.

In Russia, bombing raids were made on Sevastopol, but initially not believed when reported to the Kremlin. Later when Schulenburg delivered the declaration of war to Molotov in the Kremlin he was reported to have done so with tears in his eyes, and saying he personally believed it madness.

Within the first two days of fighting, the Luftwaffe had destroyed over 2,000 of the Soviet's airforce.

They were part of the largest invasion force the world had ever seen, with over 2,000 aircraft, 7,000 field guns and 3,350 tanks. This vast mechanised armoury was supported by 600,000 horses towing wagons and guns. Although some of the infantry were transported in vehicle, the majority of the army had to walk. The majority of the invasion went at the same pace as Napoleon's invasion in 1812. Because of the

Partisans were often well drilled and organised.

Anyone suspected of being a partisan was searched.
This picture was taken in the Orel sector early in 1943.
Even the old or the very young were considered a threat
by the Germans.

The Soviet Marshal Semyon Budenny, commander of the Soviet forces in the south and southwest of Russia at the time of initial attack on Russia. He was to prove a weak commander and had to be relieved in September 1941.

This injured commissar continues to direct the fighting.

Soviet girls assemble shells.

Russians assemble of mortars at a Siberian factory, June 1942.

enormous distances covered, wear and tear on both men and machine was considerable.

The next few days the news from the front was so bad that Stalin considered whether he should try to make peace with Hitler, almost at any price. He thought of offering the Ukraine, Belorussia and the Baltic States. On 17 October Stalin called Beria, head of NKVD (an earlier version of the KGB) and Molotov, amongst others to ask if they thought Moscow should be surrendered. Stalin made plans to evacuate Moscow but changed his mind at the last moment. Beria brought several members of his secret police, the NKVD on the streets to try and restore order. Looters panic-mongers and even drunks were shoot. To boost moral he organised a military parade and said that 'if they want a war of extermination they shall have one'.

A Soviet T-34 burns after a direct hit. The nature of this fierce

fire suggest that the engine or the fuel has been hit.

STALINGRAD

As the Kremlin was unable to contact its own Embassy in Berlin so they called in the Bulgarian ambassador Ivan Stamenov to ask if he would act as go-between. He refused and said prophetically that 'Even if you retreat to the Urals, you will still win in the end.'

It wasn't until the following day that bulk of the people in the Soviet Union became aware of the War when Molotov broadcasted on the radio to the people.

The Germans had made dramatic progress. They advanced 400 miles in the first 18 days, capturing 300,000 prisoners, 1000 tanks and 600 field guns. By 31 August they were 10 miles from the city of Leningrad. In the centre attack the Germans had taken Minsk on 30 June and Smolensk, which was only 200 miles from Moscow by mid July. Progress in the south was hampered by rainy weather and stronger

Captured Russians.

right: Part of the massive manufacturing of Soviet tanks.

above: Trains on their way to battle.

Russian assembly of anti-aircraft guns.

resistance, but the Nazi's had captured Kiev by mid-September. By the end of September more than a million prisoners had been captured.

However whilst building up Hitler's enormous military force, he had made no provision for the rapid re-supply of armoury as would be likely in a prolonged engagement. The rest of his industry was designed for keeping the troops and German nation content with consumer goods. The Russians, by contrast were less interested in supplying the people with consumer goods, but they did, however have a vast industrial capacity for the manufacture of tanks and weapons.

Hitler underestimated the number of tanks the Soviets had. He thought that they held a total of 10,000, but they actually had 24,000. They were able to manufacture twice as many tanks as the Nazis and they outclassed the main German battle tanks, in fire-power, speed and armour protection.

Hitler misunderstood the military merits of the the Blitzkrieg. The infrastructure of the western European countries (France, Belgium and Holland) were good. All of these countries together were still much smaller in land mass than Russia. Of the 850,000 miles of Russian roads, as many as 700,000 were little more than cart tracks, which became quagmires for heavy vehicles in poor weather.

The German supply lines were so stretched that the assault came to a halt. Tanks would race ahead of the main convoy and then stop as they ran out of petrol. Hitler was so sure that the campaign should be complete before winter that his armies had no winter clothing. By December over 100,000 cases of frostbite had been recorded. 14,357 men required the amputation of one or more limbs.

Partisans fighting alongside Soviet Army units engaging with the enemy on their line of retreat.

Rocket attacks by the Soviets

pound German lines.

German troops struggle against the the extreme Russian winter in 1941. Their inadequate clothing resulted in thousands of cases of frost-bite.

Soviet troops liberating Kala, November 1942.

Temperatures were as low as -56°C. However, the Russian army were well acclimatised to such extreme weather conditions and wore felt boots, fur caps and heavily quilted clothes.

The monthly losses to the Germans in the first months of the onslaught were 150,000-160,000. By November that year they had a total of 743,112 casualties, which represented almost a quarter of the total original force. However, by far the greatest losses of lives were in the Red Army where the number recorded of soldiers killed, wounded or missing was almost 5 million. A further 3 million had been taken prisoner.

Although the advancing German troops had taken 900,000 square miles of Western Russia, the Soviets had managed to evacuate over 136,000 items of heavy plant for the aviation,

A partisan attack on the Steppes.

A partisan embraces his mother, before going off to fight.

Soviet forces being given a talk by their commander on the eve of an attack.

tank, weapons and ammunition industries from the areas under attack to newly built factories in the east of the Ural Mountains. They also managed to mobilise a huge number of reserves (5 million) to replace their troops.

Stalin unleashed a massive counter offensive on the Moscow front on 6 December, refusing to let the invaders rest. The Germans were pushed back but the campaign was not decisive. The Soviet winter offensive of 1941/42 faltered by the same factors that had halted the Germans; they too were exhausted, had a lack of transport, and had problems with the ever lengthening line of communications.

General Alexander Mikahilovich Vasilevsky, who was chief of the Soviet General Staff, and along with Zhukov was co-architect of the Russian counter-offensive.

A Soviet T-26 tank in the counter attack of December 1941, is accompanied by ski-troops. A T-34 tank is in the background. The Soviets were much more adept at operating in the snow.

The snow battalions from Siberia were decisive in the Soviet counter-attack as they were well equipped, appropriately dressed and knew the terrain.

By the middle of March 1942, the Russians found themselves back on the defensive. The huge effort had left the German army basically in tact, depleted in numbers but fit enough to launch another offensive on the city of Stalingrad. The odds were stacked against the invasion from the beginning, but Hitler had become convinced in his own invincibility and overruled his more cautious generals.

Germany in 1942 was producing only 500 tanks a month, while Hitler thought it inconceivable that the Soviets could build 1200, as some reports indicated. They actually building over 2000 a month.

By the Autumn of 1942, a quarter of the Sixth Army were prisoners who had changed sides and fought with the Germans. They were known as 'Hiwis' which is short for

'Hilfswillige' meaning volunteer helper. These were divided into three categories; so called Cossack sections, which were attached to German divisions. Then there were 'Hilfswillige' which was a made up of local people and Russian prisoners who had volunteered. These wore full German Army uniforms, and had their own ranks and badges. Hitler hated the idea of Slavs in German uniforms, so they were called 'Cossacks' to make them racially acceptable for Hitler.

'Rassenkampf', is German for Racewar, which characterised this campaign. All Jews, Soviet political officers and partisans were to be taken to the SS or the Secret Field Police for usually summary execution. Historians have argued that the Wehrmacht were indoctrinated by the unprecedented propaganda into de-humanising the Soviet people. General Halder, the Chief of Staff devised the orders for collective reprisals against civilians in Russia.

Camouflaged armoury.

STALINGRAD

STALINGRAD was called Tsaritsyn, which in Tarter means town on the Tsaritsa, or yellow river. It was renamed Stalingrad when captured by Stalin during the Russian Revolution in 1917. Standing on the River Volga, it was a city full of municipal parks, tall white apartment blocks and engineering plants. Having both strategic, political and above all, psychological significance, meant that both sides would fight fiercely over this city.

General Friedrick Paulus was commander of the German sixth Army. Paulus had wanted to attack Moscow in an all out attack and capture the head of the Soviet regime. Hitler over-ruled him saying 'Moscow is of no importance'. Most German generals thought that they should first overcome the fierce resistance in Moscow. Hitler overruled them and demanded the simultaneous capture of Moscow and the Ukraine, which proved to be major strategic blunder.

German troops dug in.

By September 1942, the Nazi empire stretched from North Africa to the Arctic and from the English Channel almost to the Caspian Sea. 400 million people were under German rule.

He was attracted to the idea of attacking the south because of the rich economic and material potential of the Ukraine and the river Don basin. Hitler particularly wanted to capture the oilfields in the Caucasus and as Hitler's Army Group A comprising of the First Panzer and Seventh Armies pushed through the Caucasus they were threatened with Russian counter-attacks, particularly from Stalingrad. Hitler annoyed at the slow progress ordered the Sixth Army on 13th July to change direction and capture Stalingrad.

Hitler saw its capture on par with the southern advance and his obsession of taking the city was as strong as Stalin's

From May to September, 1942 the Germans were confident of eventual victory, as can be seen by the faces of these troops.

By September, the huge and rising casualty rate was beginning to seriously undermine both moral and the combat strength across the German army.

Russian forces attacking Stalingrad.

determination to hold on to the city that bore his name. On 28 July 1942, Stalin issued his 'not a step back' order, insisting that the city should be defended to the last man.

On 30 July the German 6th Army struck north and south of the city encircling defending Russian divisions. With the approach road to Stalingrad almost undefended, on 23 August, the 6th Army and the 4th panzer Army crossed the Don and sped towards the city.

At the time of the attack, all the population was mobilised and all men and woman aged 16-55 were called up. On the outskirts of Stalingrad, the advancing 16th panzer division were attacked by batteries which were operated by young women volunteers just out of school.

STALINGRAD

Stalingrad lay 20 miles along the high western bank of the Volga. Defenders of attack from the west had a wide stretch of water to the east from which supplies and reinforcements could come.

A massive amount of ammunition was used. The Germans used 25 million rounds in September alone. Stalin quoted Lenin 'Those who do not assist the Red Army in every way, and do not support its order and discipline are traitors and must be killed without pity.' There were 13,500 executions during the battle of Stalingrad. Deserters were sometimes shot in front of their fellow soldiers.

General Zhukov sent to Stalin a teletyped message on 10 September, saying that 'The German defensive front has been appreciably strengthened owing to the renewed movement of forces from the environs of Stalingrad itself. Further attacks with these forces and with this deployment

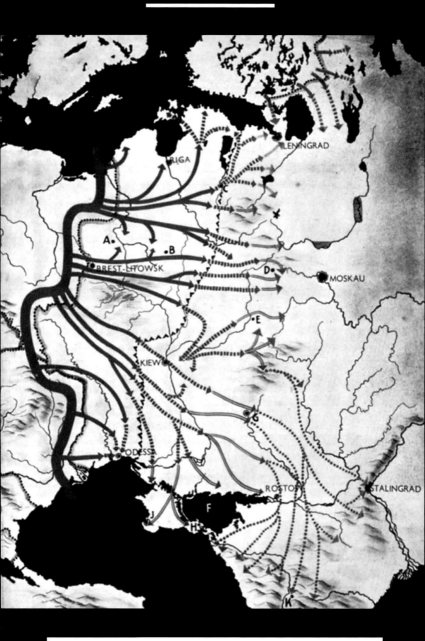

Map from the German propaganda magazine
'Signal' showing the goals of the campaign.

Paulus at the back with Hitler planning the campaign.

would be pointless, and the troops would inevitably suffer heavy losses. We need reinforcements and time to regroup for a more concentrated frontal assault. Thrusts by individual armies are not sufficient to dislodge the enemy.'

The Russians used T-34 tanks preferring them to the American tanks which had thinner protection. Rodimtsev counter attacked with Me-109s. During intense fighting in Stalingrad, the main railway station changed hands 15 times in 5 days.

Russian women served in several all female units. These units were with the so called partisans. They also served as gunners, spies, in medical corps and the auxiliary services, as well as fighting on the front line.

above: A German plane is shot down.

left: Soviet forces marching across the frozen Steepes.

Richthofen gave all the Fourth Air Fleet's to be diverted to the Stalingrad front totalling 1200 aircraft including Junkers 88, Heinkel 111 bombers as well as Stukas for the Stalingrad attack on Sunday 23 August 1942. Flames from damaged petrol storage tanks rose 1500 feet in the air. Richthofen was first to use carpet bombing in Guernica in the Spanish Civil War.

The fourth fleet flew 1,600 sorties dropping 1,000 tons of bombs for the loss of 3 aircraft. Estimates are that 40,000 of Stalingrad's citizens were killed in the first week of bombardment.

The Germans had the 6th Army and the 4th Panzer Army facing along a 400-mile front a huge Soviet army equal to their own. Both had 590,000 men, but the Germans had more tanks, artillery and aircraft. Preceding the attack for 24 hours, the Germans used massive air raids on Stalingrad. At 0630 on 13 September the Germans launched their attack with an onslaught with the aim of overrunning the the Southern half of the city. The Russians replied with 10,000 rounds a day from their Katyusha rocket launchers.

Stalin in Moscow order Stalingrad to be held and fresh reserves were rushed to the city. Hitler then ordered his panzer forces south and when he recalled them two weeks later, Stalingrad had been reinforced.

The Russians held firm until the 14th, when troops of the 76th Infantry Division, with tanks broke through. But they were unable to hold the city and in mid-September 1942 large numbers of German forces entered the city and fighting became street-by-street and house-by-house, something the Germans were unaccustomed to and hated. By mid October the Germans had captured the southern and central force of the city and were trying to take the industrial northern sections. The Soviets appeared trapped and casualty rates reached their peak as savage hand to hand fighting took place, in which few prisoners were taken from each side. The Germans now nicknamed the war 'Rattenkrieg' (a war of the rats). This war of attrition was to last 80 days and 80 nights, using up all of the divisions Paulus possessed.

On 27 September Hitler made a speech to commemorate the 1923 Putsch which was broadcast across Germany and to the troops in Stalingrad. 'I wanted to get to the Volga and to do so at a particular point where stands a certain town. By chance it bears the name of Stalin himself. I wanted to take the place, and do you know, modest as we are, we've pulled it off, we've got it really, except for a few enemy positions holding out. Now people say: 'Why don't they finish the job more quickly?' Well, the reason is that I don't want another Verdun. I prefer to do the job with quite small assault groups. Times of no consequence at all.' He also had earlier said

Storming the last remaining enemy strongholds in Stalingrad, January 1943.

Soviet partisans advancing along side tanks.

'Where the German soldier sets foot, there he remains...You my rest assured that nobody will ever drive us away from Stalingrad.' Hitler's obsession meant that the lives of thousands of German soldiers were to be thrown away as a point of principle.

On 2nd October, Paulus was demanding that his troops capture Stalingrad as quickly as possible on the grounds that Hitler had said that it was 'urgently necessary for psychological reasons' because Communism must be 'deprived of its shrine.'

General Zhukov had meanwhile been gathering reserves around the city and on 19th November he counter-attacked under Generals A.M.Vasilevsky and N.N. Voronov. By the end of November the Germans were themselves trapped. Paulus wanted to retreat, but Hitler refused in spite of the general's increasingly desperate calls.

top: Field Marshal Bock, who unsuccessfully tried to stop the
mass escape of Soviet forces across the Don, July, 1942

left: A more confident Paulus at the being of the campaign.

General Rokossovsky awaits the opening of 'Operation Ring', on 10th January 1943. 7,000 field guns mortars and launchers attacked for fifty-five minutes.

The Rumanians at the rear were close to collapse and the German 6th army would then be surrounded. Paulus and Hoth regularly sent reports saying that large numbers of Russian troops were amassing, but through Hitler's obstinacy, they were unable to make a tactical retreat.

Salvoes of Katyushas, which were Russian rockets fired from multiple rocket launchers were fired before major onslaughts. The German troops called them 'Stalin's Organs.'

Reinforcements arrived from Germany and they had massive air support with 3,000 sorties being flown in one day. The Germans fought with an added sense of desperation as the dreaded Russian winter was once more soon to arrive.

The German tank, nicknamed the Rhino.

URANUS

THE CAREFULLY PLANNED Soviet trap, Operation Uranus began on the 19 November to 23 November. The southern front was 280 miles long and under the command of General Yeremenko, and had four armies and 383,981 men, including the 62 army under Chuikov in Stalingrad itself.

The Don front was 93 miles long and under General Rokossovsky and had 292,707 men.

The South western Front was 154 miles long and under the command of General Vatutin and had a total of 338,631 men. The total army numbered 1,015,299 ready for the counter attack.

Paulus in November 1942 surveying Russian positions through periscope binoculars.

The weakest link of the German army were the Rumanian forces under the command of General Dumitrescu and about 100,000 men. They were less well equipped, moral was low and their horse-drawn 37mm guns were ineffective against Russian tanks. On 19 November 1942 on, a very cold foggy morning, the counter-attack began. No aircraft were needed as the weather was too cold. A 90 mile gap had opened on the axis front. As the Russians swept deeper into the German rear, Zeitzler tried in vain to persuade Hitler to allow a tactical withdrawal.

On the Southern front, 24 hours after the the Northern front defence position were attacked, 1,320 guns at 10.00 attacked and within 2 hours the Rumanians had suffered 35,000 casualties, killed, wounded or taken prisoner. Hitler was in the Berghoff in Bavaria and was asked to allow the 6th army to counter-attack and break out, but he again refused. His

The German infantry had to fight hand-to-hand in much of Stalingrad, using such weapons as the Mauser M98K rifle an MP38/40 sub-machine gun and hand grenades.

The troops shown here are are clearly under strain as they prepare to take the Barrikady Factory, in October 1942.

Nazis retreating through the snow.

reason was that 'if we abandon the Stalingrad, we are really abandoning the whole meaning of the campaign.'

Paulus and Schmidt regularly took to the air to review the unfolding disaster. They realised that it would be totally impractical to supply their 6th army by an airlift. The river Don had now frozen and could be crossed. Paulus wished to make a South Westerly break out to reach the nearest German forces outside the encirclement, but again Hitler would not be persuaded. The Rumanians had after five days run out of ammunition and the promised re-supplies by air did not materialise, as promised by Hitler. The temperature was 30-40 degrees of frost and on the 22 November a desperate Paulus with fuel and ammunition running low, had planned a break out, but Hitler refused. Hitler instead offered a below strength panzer division, but this would take two weeks to arrive and in any case not make much difference.

Hitler began to look for some one to blame and held General Heim responsible. He was arrested and imprisoned, but quietly released later in the war.

Hitler put great faith in any new weapon and hoped that his formidable Tiger tank which was coming off the production line would have dramatic effect and break the encirclement. However there were only 45 available.

Göering convinced Hitler that his airforce, the Luftwaffe could supply the 500 tons of supplies necessary by airlift. This was against the advice of the other generals, most

Katyusha rocket-launchers signalling the start of the Russian assault on the Rumanian positions.

By November to December, when the weather had become poor, they were encircled and running out of supplies, they were beginning to die of the cold or malnutrition.

noticeably Zeitzler who backed Paulus. This impossible task could only be achieved by 375 JU-52 transport planes each carrying two tons, taking off each day. Because of the poor weather, only 30-35 could be relied upon, meaning a total of 1,050 planes were actually required for the task. There were only 750 JU-52 planes in existence and these were all over Europe and North Africa. From 25-29 November there were only 47 available which could manage an average of 53.8 tons of supplies. This being just over 10% of what was actually required. Of these 17 were lost in action and by 17 December they were 7,064 tons short and the Germans were soon suffering from malnutrition. Field-Marshal Erich von Manstein was given the task of breaking through, but was given no sizable force with which to so do.

Hand-to-hand fighting, in the Red October factory, Stalingrad, winter, 1943. overleaf: A quite break in the fighting.

The Wasp, on a panzer II chassis.

Russians IL-2 planes in production, 1942.

Manstein, who tried through his messengers
to persuade Paulus to break out.

SATURN

STALIN BEGAN Operation Saturn on 16 December and his artillery attacked enemy positions for 90 minutes along two hundred miles. Then the main attack fell upon General Gariboldi's 8th Italian Army, which had 216,000 men in eleven divisions, defending some 130 miles. For three days they put up a fierce resistance and then retreated in to the foggy snowy steppe. Manstein ordered his intelligence chief, a Major Eismann to fly into Stalingrad and persuade Paulus and Schmidt that a break out was the only option. Both rejected the proposal, partly because it would be over ruling Hitler's orders. When Manstein established a direct link with Paulus he agreed that 'At present rate of supply it will not be possible to hold the Kessel much longer.'

General Konstantin Rokossovsky who commanded the Soviet armies of the Don front and launched the final offensive on the 6th January.

Field Marshal Göering controlled the Luftwaffe and his lack of air support contributed to the capitulation of the Sixth Army. The German Stalingrad troops used to say that the overweight Göering should be put on a 'Stalingrad diet'. Many of the German high command had fought in Russia in World War One and so they were not unfamiliar with the conditions that they were to face. However all planning had been for a short campaign. Hoth attempted one last attack to try and break through, but this was repulsed.

The men of the 6th Army quickly realised that the end was drawing to close. On Christmas day, they listened to a radio broadcast by Goebbels, in which supposedly German soldiers in Stalingrad were singing a rendition of 'Stille Nacht' (Silent Night).

The German Tiger tanks which came too late to save Stalingrad, were built to counter the Soviet T-34 and KV-1. They were impervious to almost all Russian guns, unless they were fired at very close range. It fired a deadly 88mm gun, and the manufacturers claimed that it was completely accurate at one thousand meters.

Russians fighting in the rubble of Stalingrad.

General Georgi Konstantinovich Zhukov, the Deputy Supreme Commander of the Red Army.

Field Marshal von Manstein, who was recognised as one of the German Army's most able strategists. He was unable to halt the Russian advance and relieve Paulus and the 6th Army.

The well-kitted out Soviet infantry prepares to attack the German troops in the rubble of Stalingrad.

overleaf: German troops lie dead and dying after a combat.

The Army had suffered 28,000 casualties, mostly from enemy action, but a large number of men were suddenly dying from non-violent causes. A pathologist was flown in to conduct an autopsy and concluded that the soldiers had prematurely senile bodies because of the privations. Their meagre diet was less than 1000 calories a day. Their watery soup was often only supplemented with bones from the corpses of horses that they dug up.

Hitler was indifferent to their plight. In the week leading up to Christmas a number of the few transport planes which were sent to Stalingrad only contained Christmas trees, when the men were starving to death.

On New Years eve, the Russian artillery launched fired a volley of shots skywards to welcome in the the New Year.

These soviet troops are adopting the heroic pose for the camera. The two soldiers in helmets are armed with PPSh sub-machine guns, and the comrade in the side-hat is aiming with a 1928 DP light machine gun. Although the Germans had taken large sections of the city, small parts of city were never captured and in the counter attack, they were ill- equipped at fighting at close range.

left: Evacuating the wounded from the field of battle.

Front-line in Karelia, November 1942.

top: Soviet artillery launches an attack.

Hitler sent a New Years day message to the soldiers saying that 'The men of the Sixth Army have my word that everything is being done to extradite them,' which meant little to the soldiers who felt that they were abandoned.

The Russians then launched a massive air assault with 7,000 piece of artillery.

Voronov, after establishing a radio link sent two officers, Major Smyslov and Captain Dyatlenko to deliver an ultimatum to the 6th Army; to surrender or die.

Paulus relayed the demand to Hitler, who replied that 'every day the Army holds out helps Eastern Front since Russian divisions are kept away from it.'

Relentless fighting in the suburbs of Stalingrad, 1942.

Surrounded German troops under fire from Soviet forces, January 1943.

The Russians launched a sustained attack on the 10 January. Hitler tried to send 300 tons of supplies a day, hoping to keep the 6th Army fit enough to fight another 6-8 weeks. But only 15 out of the total of 140 Ju-52s were operational. There was only one poor airstrip open and so during the five day period only 60 tons were delivered. On Friday, 22 January, the Russians launched another massive onslaught on the German positions. To give some idea of the scale of this attack, 24,000,000 rounds of machine-gun and rifle rounds were spent, along with 911,00 artillery rounds and 990,000 mortar shells. That night Paulus radioed to Hitler that: 'Rations exhausted... What orders should I give to troops who have no more ammunition and are subject to mass attacks by heavy artillery fire? The quickest decision is necessary since disintegration is already starting in some places.'

Cavalry charge by Soviet forces.

Russians in winter clothing in Stalingrad attack, 1942.

overleaf: Fierce fighting within Stalingrad.

Hitler replied 'Surrender is out of the question. The troops will defend themselves to the last. If possible, the size of the fortress is to be reduced so that it can be held by troops still capable of fighting. The courage and endurance of the fortress have made it possible to establish a new front and begin preparing a counter-operation. Thereby, Sixth Army has made an historic contribution to Germany's greatest single struggle.'

Paulus was not given permission to break out of his entrapment and the promised resupply by the Luftwaffe was to little and too late. Hitler had issued a Führer directive saying that sixth Army Corps must 'resist to the last to tie down as much enemy as possible to facilitate operations from the fronts.' In all 91,000 Axis prisoners were to be taken including twenty-two German generals.

above: Troops outside the ruined buildings.

left: Soviet forces also used flame throwers. This photograph was taken in December 1942.

Russians crossing the frozen Volga.

Preparing for the attack on Stalingrad.

Heinrich Himmler, the organiser of the SS and Gestapo.

General Kurt Zeitzler, who tried unsuccessfully to persuade Hitler to allow the 6th Army to break out of the encirclement in Stalingrad.

STALINGRAD

Hitler on hearing of the coming final collapse made Paulus a Field-Marshal and promoted several others to the rank of Major-General. Paulus effusively thanked Hitler, apparently unaware that he was supposed to commit suicide rather than be taken prisoner, as no German Field-Marshal had ever been taken prisoner.

The 6th Army was split into two. With the Soviets within a few hundred yards, at 7.15 a.m on 31 January, Paulus, by then isolated and ill, surrendered. A 21 year old, Lieutenant Ilchenko, took the surrender. As he left his headquarters Paulus said to General Pfeffer 'I have no intention of shooting myself for this Bohemian corporal.'

When he knew that Paulus had not killed himself, Hitler had said 'This hurts me so much because the heroism of so many

When all provisions had run out, the encircled Germans slaughtered and ate horse-meat.

Soviets in house to house fighting.

overleaf: Combat in the snow.

soldiers is nullified by one single characterless weakling... What is life? Life is nation. The individual must die anyway... What hurts me most, personally, is that I still promoted him to Field-Marshal. I wanted to give him this final satisfaction. He could have freed himself from all sorrow and ascended into eternity and national immortality, but he prefers to go to Moscow.'

As the 6th Army had been broken in to two halves by the Soviets, the remaining troops did not surrender until 2nd February 1943.

When the rest of the 6th Army surrendered, they did with starving troops. The army's exact losses were difficult to ascertain but it is thought that 300,000 men died in the battle for Stalingrad. Amazingly, 9,796 civilians had managed to live through the fighting, surviving in the ruined houses. Such was the loss of lives that bodies were being still dug up around Stalingrad for decades afterwards.

Soviet troops march towards Stalingrad.

154

Soviet forces enter Stalingrad at the end of the siege.

German troop digs in for the final assault.

The Soviet T-34 tank.

Artillery training fire upon Nazi aircraft which have broken through Soviet defences. By the end of the battle, few German aircraft were able to land. Supplies, which were delivered by the Luftwaffe in heavy bomb-canisters, often fell wide of the two German pockets. Even when the Germans knew where they had fallen, they were often too exhausted to retrieve them.

STALINGRAD

All the captured Generals were reasonably healthy, with the exception of Paulus, who was ill and had developed a nervous tick on his left cheek. Of the the 91,000 prisoners nearly half were dead within a few months. Typhus was a major killer. An unknown number were shot out of hand, others died of gangrene. Although the Soviets knew surrender of the 6th Army was imminent, no preparations for rations had been made. When rations did arrive after three or for days, many of the prisoners had not eaten for two weeks. These rations were a loaf of bread between ten men, plus some soup made from millet and salted fish. The Wehrmacht's record on the treatment of it's own prisoners was also incredibly harsh.

The Soviets separated senior military personnel from the rest of the army and they were given shelter and better food. For the rest of the prisoners, there would often be no shelter at night. Prisoners slept in the snow, huddled together for warmth. The following morning, there would be several new corpses.

The Germans hated the hand-to-hand fighting that they were forced to fight once in Stalingrad.

Russians fighting in the suburbs of Stalingrad, 1942.

Both German and Rumanian soldiers resorted to cannibalism to stay alive. Slices were cut from corpses and boiled up which was called 'camel-meat' Those who ate it became recognisable because they started to regain their complexions, instead of the grey pallor of the majority. The Soviets claimed that 'only at gun-point could prisoners be forced to desist from this barbarism.' The large and powerfully built prisoners were the first to die, as the meagre rations were the same for all, as size was of no consequence. Only the horses had their rations altered according to their size. The prisoners were set to work all over the Soviet Union. When some prisoners were sent to work on a power station, they found that no huts were available to live in only earth bunkers. Moltov stated that no prisoners would see their homes until Stalingrad was rebuilt. One of the first buildings to be repaired was the NKVD headquarters.

left: Field Marshal von Paulus surrenders, accompanied by General Arthur Schmidt and Colonel Wilhelm Adam. February 1st 1943.

Paulus had been suffering from nervous exhaustion and had been laying ill for some days, prior to surrender.

Paulus and Schmidt in captivity.

The collapse of the Stalingrad front and the virtual annihilation of the 4th and 6th armies represented the biggest defeat in German history. It also brought to Germany new mood of desperation. Presenting this military catastrophe to the German people involved Goebbels using all his skills in propaganda. He tried to portray the defeat as 'heroic' and failed to mention that 91,000 soldiers had been taken prisoner. He actually forbad the delivery of postcards from the prisoner of war camps as he claimed it would promote 'Bolshevik propaganda.' In the end the Russians dropped leaflets from the prisoners on German front lines, which were forwarded on by the German troops, at great personal risk to themselves.

Goebbels also demanded mass mobilisation, copper cladding from the Bradenburg gate was removed for use in the war. Luxury shops such as jewellers were closed along with fashion magazines, nightclubs and luxury restaurants.

Rumanian troops after capture.

This well clothed German prisoner eats from a large loaf of bread. The truth for many was very different.

A column of German prisoners taken into captivity after their surrender in Stalingrad. Of the 91,000 prisoners captured, only 5,000 were to ever see Germany again. They had to contend with appaling conditions in captivity, some who had to sleep in the open snow, would huddle together to keep warm. Although some were arbitrarily executed, most died through the cold, undernourishment or illness.

As soon as Stalingrad was final retaken by the Soviets, they waved the red flag from one of the few remaining buildings. These photographs were a valuable morale booster for the allies and were symbolic of the changing fortunes for the two sides.

n the name of the people of the United States of America, I present this scroll to the City of Stalingrad to commemorate our admiration for its gallant defenders whose courage, fortitude, and devotion during the siege of September 13, 1942 to January 31, 1943 will inspire forever the hearts of all free people. Their glorious victory stemmed the tide of invasion and marked the turning point in the war of the Allied Nations against the forces of aggression.

May 17ᵗʰ 1944

Franklin D. Roosevelt

Washington, D.C.

Bartering became common. Germany finally switched to being a command economy, years after Britain, which had been preparing for a possible conflict as early as the late 1930s .

By 1945 3,000 of the Stalingrad prisoners had been released usually because they were not fit for labour. By 1955 there were still 9,626 German prisoners of war in Russia and it was not until Chancellor Adenauer's visit to Moscow in that year, that they were finally set free. These included Generals Schmidt, Seydlitz and Rosenburg and Lieutenant Gottfried von Bismark.

Paulus wife died in 1947 in Baden-Baden, without ever having seen her husband since the war. Finally released by the Soviets in the autumn of 1953, he died in 1957 in Dresden, East Germany. He was buried next to his wife in Baden-Baden.

The collapse of the Stalingrad front was a crushing blow for the Nazi regime. Particularly since Hitler had made so public his personal commitment to keeping the city. After the fall, there were attempts at propaganda such as this cover of 'Signal' which tried to give a heroic gloss to the dramatic change in the balance of the war.

Captured Germans paraded through the streets of Moscow.

German military equipment captured in battles, being inspected by Soviets, just outside Stalingrad, February 1943.

All that was left of Stalingrad after the the battle.

Stalingrad after it was rebuilt.

Stalingrad became a city of the dead. Such were the numbers of deaths, that only a few had proper burials. Most were simply put into mass graves.